Contents

Introduction

Heat is a form of energy. On Earth, most of our heat energy comes from the Sun, even though it is 92 million miles away.

thermometer

The temperature scale most used in science is Celsius (°C). Water boils at 100 °C, and freezes at 0 °C. The lowest possible temperature where no heat energy at all remains is –273.15 °C, known as **absolute zero**. It is a theoretical point that can't quite be reached, but scientists can get very close to it! We make a thermometer on page 20.

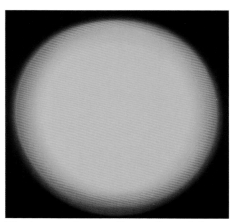

The temperature on the surface of the Sun is about 5500 °C.

Pompeii worm

All forms of life need heat to survive, but not always the same amount. In the frozen soils of Alaska and Siberia, there are tiny life forms called microbes which survive and grow in temperatures well below freezing (–20 °C). Meanwhile, under the sea, around deep ocean vents, the Pompeii worm lives and thrives in water at 80 °C. How does the walrus cope with freezing sea temperatures? See our experiment on page 16.

Heat energy can move from one place to another in different ways. Look at our experiments on conduction, convection and radiation.

hot air balloon

radiant heater

heat conductors inside a computer

Some technical or unusual words, shown in *italic* type, are explained in the glossary on page 31.

Materials and tools

For our experiments, you may have to buy a few things from a shop but you should easily find most of what you need around the home.

20 minutes

This tells you about how long a project could take.

This symbol means you might need adult help.

Wire You will need fairly thin, flexible wire. It's usually available in hardware stores. You can also use the kind of garden wire that's used for securing plants.

Kettle Ask to use an old kettle if you can – either an electric kettle or one you can heat up on a stove. You will need an adult to help.

Glue stick This is mostly used for sticking paper to paper. Universal glue is a rubbery stuff that sticks most things to most other things!

Hair dryer Ask before you borrow this and use it with care. It's an instant source of hot air.

Clock You'll need one that shows seconds to help record time in some of the experiments. Put your timings in a notebook to compare results.

Tape We use sticky tape to hold things in position. Masking tape or clear parcel tape will do.

Night light Always use with care, and never leave lighted candles unattended. Beware of hot wax. Follow our instructions exactly.

Scissors Ask an adult for a safe pair of scissors that you can use for your experiments.

Oven glove Always use padded gloves if you are handling anything hot. Avoid painful burns!

Tubes Collect cardboard tubes from kitchen towels or other paper rolls to use in experiments.

Thread Strong sewing cotton is called thread. Ask permission to use some from the work basket.

Thermometer Sometimes these are used in cooking, so you may find one in the kitchen.

Ice lolly sticks Keep them to use in the experiments.

Kitchen foil Aluminium cooking foil usually comes on cardboard rolls. Keep any old rolls, we'll need them later.

Matches Try to get extra long matches. They're often sold as 'cooks matches'. Take care!

Mugs You will probably find everyday mugs in the kitchen. Don't use your mother's best china!

Foam cups Keep any plastic cups you may get with take-aways, they will be useful for our experiments.

Cutlery Ask permission before you use knives and forks. Most homes have old cutlery in a kitchen drawer.

Bubble wrap Bubbles of air are sealed between layers of thin plastic sheet. It's mostly used for packaging, but we use it for insulation.

Freezer Always ask permission if you need to use the freezer. Perhaps an adult can clear a space or a drawer for you to use.

Saucepan Use an old cooking pan if possible. You should ask an adult to help you use the stove.

Tissue paper It's often used for wrapping presents or glassware, and is available from craft shops in sheets of different colours.

Food dye Small bottles of food dyes are available from supermarkets for colouring cakes and sweets. It's very strong. You will only need a few drops.

Plasticine If you don't already have some of this popular modelling material, you can get it from a good craft shop.

Friends can help Do the experiments with your friends!

Salt You'll need quite a lot of salt for your experiments!

Ice cubes Collect together some ice cubes from your freezer tray, put them in a plastic bag then back into the freezer, ready for use in experiments.

Straws We'll need some drinking straws. Try the kitchen drawer!

Plastic bottles Ask an adult for empty plastic bottles. The ones used for water and soft drinks are best.

Sandwich bags You'll need some plastic sandwich bags for your margarine experiment!

Shoe box Every time someone has new shoes, there might be a box available. Save them for experiments.

Card Cut thin card from old cereal boxes to save buying sheets from the art shop!

Conduction

Conduction is the way heat is carried through solid materials, for example, from a kitchen hob through the saucepan to the food.

The plan

We are going to find out which materials are best at conducting heat.

You will need:

- hot water (kettle)
- mug
- assortment of long, thin objects made of different materials, such as:
  table forks and spoons
  wire coat hanger
  plastic straw
  knitting needles
- clock that shows seconds

What to do:

1 Heat some water in a kettle.

2 Put some hot water in the mug. Be careful!

3 Stand the first object in the water. Hold the other end. See how long it takes to become too hot to hold.

4 Fill the mug with hot water again and try other things. This time we're testing a metal coat hanger.

5 Now it's a plastic drinking straw.

6 This is a wooden spoon.

What's going on?

Energy in the form of heat passes from one molecule to the next along the object. Metals conduct heat well and so are called good conductors. Non-metals, like plastics and wood, are not good conductors and are called *insulators*.

What else can you do?

Try comparing results for objects made of the same material, but of different thicknesses.

Jargon Buster
A **molecule** is the smallest unit of a compound.

Convection

The way that heat is carried through liquids and gases, for example, a radiator heating up a whole room, is called *convection*.

The plan

We are going to show a convection current in air by using *smoke*.

You will need:

- shoe box with a lid
- two kitchen roll tubes
- night light in a holder
- one lolly stick
- sticky tape
- thin card
- thread

What to do:

1 Draw two circles on the lid of the shoe box, one towards each end. Draw round the end of the kitchen roll tube.

2 Cut the holes out and stick the tubes in place with sticky tape.

3 Light the night light and put it in the shoebox so that it is under one of the tubes when the lid goes on.

4 Light the end of the lolly stick with a match. (Ask an adult to help.) Then blow the flame out.

5 Hold the glowing stick over the tube that doesn't have the night light under it.

6 Smoke goes down the tube and eventually comes out of the other.

What's going on?

The candle flame heats the air, which rises up through the tube. Cooler air is heavier and is drawn down the other tube. Air travels through the box, drawing the smoke with it.

What else can you do?

Copy this *spiral* shape onto thin card and cut it out with scissors. Attach a thread to the middle and hang it up. Put a night light under it – not closer than 200 mm (8 in) – and watch the rising air make it spin!

Don't put the night light too close!

11

Radiation

30 minutes

Radiation is another way that heat travels through gases. Heat can also travel through a *vacuum* by radiation. An example is the way heat gets to us from the Sun, through space.

The plan

We are going to show how different substances absorb heat radiation.

You will need:

- thermometer
- desk lamp
- different, contrasting materials: for example, things that are light or dark, shiny or matt, cut into pieces of a similar size and shape
- sticky tape

Experiment 1

The lamp produces heat as well as light.

1 Find a place to work where the *temperature* is fairly even. Keep away from direct sunlight and room heaters.

2 We are using a desk lamp as a source of radiant heat. Put your thermometer under the lamp.

3 Note the temperature rise after ten minutes.

What's going on?

Heat is getting to the thermometer by radiation. It is a way in which heat travels as waves of energy.

Experiment 2

Keep the lamp at the same distance from the thermometer.

1 Start with the thermometer at room temperature again. Wrap it in a fold of test material. This is kitchen foil, which is very thin aluminium sheet. Hold it in place with sticky tape.

2 Put the wrapped thermometer under the lamp. Note the temperature after 10 minutes, then at 10-minute intervals.

3 Let the thermometer cool back to room temperature, then repeat with other materials. You can try combinations, too!

4 Make a graph to show your results. It should show that shiny material insulates against radiant heat better than matt. Lighter material insulates better than darker material.

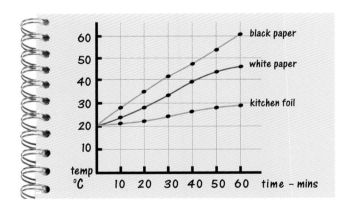

What's going on?

Dark, matt surfaces absorb these waves and soak up the heat. Light, shiny surfaces reflect the waves and stay cooler.

What else can you do?

Can radiation pass through solids? Try putting a sheet of card, glass or plastic between the radiator and the thermometer.

Jargon Buster

Radiant heat is heat given off by something hot. **Radiation** is a general word used for energy that travels in waves. **Radiator** describes something that gives off energy. The radiators in our homes give off heat by a mixture of radiation and convection.

Insulation

Insulation is a quality a material has when it does not easily allow heat to pass through it.

The plan

We are going to show how different materials can cut down heat loss.

You will need:

- some material to use as insulation, such as bubble wrap, kitchen foil, cardboard, plastic sheet (cut from plastic bags), felt, sponge cloth, paper
- at least five foam plastic cups
- a few other cups or mugs – about the same size as the insulated ones
- thermometer
- pencil and paper
- clock that shows seconds

What to do:

paper   bubble   sponge
tin foil   plastic

1 Set up at least five foam plastic cups and two made of other materials.

2 Cut discs of different materials to make covers for the cups. Make combinations of materials, too.

3 Put the lids on the cups they are to go on. Make a note of which is which on labels.

4 Heat up water in a kettle. When it's quite hot, pour some water into each of the containers.

5 Take the temperature in each cup, then quickly put its cover on.

6 Note the water temperature in each cup on a graph.

7 Wait for 10 minutes. Take the temperature in each cup again. Stir the water before taking the reading.

8 Plot points on your graph. Repeat at 10 minute intervals. The more times you do this, the better.

What's going on?

With no cover, heat is quickly lost to the air. Layers containing trapped air are better insulators. The best cover combined a layer of kitchen foil, which stopped radiant heat, with a layer of kitchen towel, which contained air – a bad heat conductor.

What else can you do?

Look around your home to find examples of insulation at work. Look at the different materials in your clothes.

Jargon Buster
Bubble wrap is a plastic sheet with sealed bubbles of air all over it.

Keeping warm

25 minutes

How does a walrus stay warm? Have you ever seen a skinny walrus or a seal that isn't wobblingly obese? No? Let's find out why by making a *blubber* mitten!

You will need:

- supply of thin plastic sandwich bags
- soft *margarine* at room temperature
- washing-up bowl
- ice cubes, spoons
- hair *stretchies*, string or wool to put around your wrists
- watch or clock that shows seconds
- assistant

The plan

You're going to find out for yourself how well fat works as an insulator.

What to do:

1 Scoop margarine into a plastic bag.

2 Put one hand into another plastic bag. Use your left hand if you're right-handed, or your right hand if you're left-handed.

3 Spread a thick layer of margarine over the bag. Now put this hand into the bag that already has margarine in and squish the margarine around so that it covers your hand. This is your 'blubber mitten'.

4 Ask your friend to fasten the mitten with elastic bands or 'stretchies' so that they don't slip off – but not too tight. Put two empty plastic bags on the other hand and fasten these, too.

5 Fill the bowl with cold water and ice cubes.

6 Put both hands into the ice water. Don't let water into the bags. Use the watch to time how long you can keep each hand in the water before it gets uncomfortable.

What's going on?

The margarine insulates, keeping the warmth of your hand in rather than letting it pass to the water. Animals that live in very cold areas have thick layers of fat under their skin to keep their bodies warm. You feel cold because heat goes from your hand – not because cold comes from the water!

What else can you do?

You could try wearing a woollen or padded glove on the hand that doesn't have the blubber mitten. Use a plastic bag to keep it dry. Can you keep the hand in for longer than with just a bag? Which is a better insulator, blubber or the fabric glove?

The water cycle

Nature has its own water recycling system we call the water *cycle*.

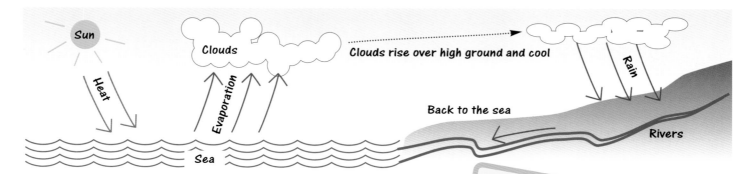

Sun

Heat

Clouds

Evaporation

Clouds rise over high ground and cool

Rain

Back to the sea

Rivers

Sea

The plan

We are going to see how water *evaporates* and condenses.
Then we're going to make our own *clouds*!

You will need:

- kettle
- hand mirror
- oven gloves
- clear, one-litre plastic bottle
- matches
  (long ones would be best)

What to do:

1 Fill a kettle half full of water and start heating it.

2 When it begins to boil, turn the kettle off, and use the oven gloves to hold the mirror in the steam.

3 You should soon see water droplets form on the surface of the mirror.

What's going on?

The element in the kettle heats the water until it starts to change from a liquid (water) to a vapour (steam). The steam is less dense than water and takes up more space, so it pushes its way out of the kettle. Steam touching the surface of the mirror is quickly cooled, and changes back to water.

What else can you do?

water level

1 Put enough warm water in a bottle to cover the bottom. Light a match and let it burn for a few seconds before blowing it out.

2 Immediately, hold the match in the neck of the bottle to catch as much smoke as you can.

cloud shapes

3 Quickly put the cap on the bottle so as not to lose any smoke.

4 Squeeze the bottle eight or nine times (more may be necessary).

5 When you release the bottle, you should see little clouds forming inside.

What's going on?

Some of the warm water evaporates inside the bottle. Releasing the pressure in the bottle slightly cools the air inside so some of the water vapour changes back to liquid droplets. The smoke particles help them to form. Clouds are just collections of water droplets.

Jargon Buster
A **droplet** is a very small drop of liquid. A **particle** is a very small amount of something solid.

Expansion

25 minutes

When things get bigger they are said to expand.
Things expand when they are heated and when they
are cooled, they contract, or get smaller.

The plan

We are going to make our own thermometer.

You will need:

- plastic bottle
- plastic drinking straw
- plasticine, thermometer
- warm water
- food dye
- saucepan, stove

This thermometer is
made of glass and
plastic. It has a
special red liquid
inside it.

plasticine seal

1 Fill the bottle to the brim with cool, dyed water.

2 Seal the straw into the neck with plasticine, with
most of the straw outside the bottle.

The water has risen from here

to here!

3 Put the bottle in a saucepan of warm water. Heat moves from the water in the pan to the water in the bottle. Water rises up the straw a little.

4 Gently heat the pan. Get an adult to help you with this. As the water in the pan gets hotter, the water rises higher in the straw.

What's going on?

When the water is heated, it expands. The only way it can go is up the straw. The hotter it becomes, the more it expands, so the further up the straw it goes.

What else can you do?

Compare your thermometer with a commercial one. Make sure it's the kind that can go into very hot water. Use the readings from the commercial thermometer to label your new thermometer.

Jargon Buster

We **calibrate** a thermometer by comparing it to a standard one and putting the temperature marks in the right places.

-40°

-30°

-20°

Solid water

24 hours

In the last section, we said that most things contract when they cool. Well, when water *freezes* it expands!

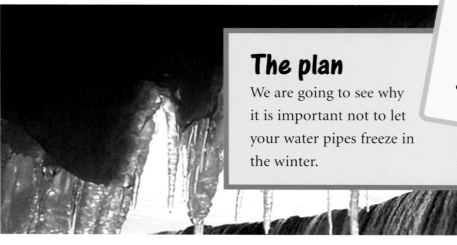

The plan

We are going to see why it is important not to let your water pipes freeze in the winter.

You will need:

- 2 large plastic bottles
- 1 small plastic bottle
- water
- freezer

Experiment 1

1 Fill the bottle to the top with cold water and fasten the cap.

2 Place it in the freezer and leave it there overnight.

bulge in bottle

3 By the next morning, the bottle will be swollen. It may even have split open!

22

What's going on?

When water freezes, it forms ice crystals which occupy more space than water molecules. For the same volume, ice is less dense than water. Water is very unusual in this. Most liquids become more dense as they cool. Water is at its most dense at 4 °*Celsius*.

An *iceberg* is lighter than the water it floats in, so that one-tenth of it is above the water.

Experiment 2

How can we check that one-tenth of floating ice is above the water? Iceberg shapes are very hard to measure!

4-6   8-12

base of ice block

1 Use two plastic bottles, one a little smaller than the other. They need to be fairly straight-sided. Cut the top off the larger one. The smaller one should just fit inside it.

2 Fill the smaller one with water, but only as far as where it starts to narrow. Place it in the freezer overnight, standing upright.

3 In the morning, get an adult to help you cut the bottle off the ice with scissors. Put some water in the larger bottle and float the ice block in it. You can now measure how much is standing out of the water.

Jargon Buster
Ice and steam are both water, but in different **states**.

Antifreeze?

Have you ever wondered why we put salt on the roads when it's icy or snowing?

24 hours

The plan

We are going to see what effect adding salt to water has on the way it freezes.

You will need:

- two similar plastic bottles with screw tops
- mixing jug, spoon
- water, salt
- freezer
- short piece of thread

Experiment 1

plain water →

← salt solution

1 Make some salt solution. Add salt to water until no more will *dissolve*.

2 Fill a bottle to the top with salt water and another with the same amount of plain cold water. Put them both in the freezer overnight.

3 In the morning, only the plain water has frozen.

plain water →

What's going on?
Impurities in water, in this case salt, lower the freezing point so the water remains liquid.

Experiment 2
Here's a little trick you can try using ice.

1 Put a cube of ice in a glass of plain water.

2 Pour a little salt onto the cube.

3 Hang the end of a piece of thread so that it lies on the salty patch and leave it for a few minutes.

4 After a while, you'll be able to pick up the cube with the thread! Can you work out what's going on?

Jargon Buster
A **solution** is a mixture of two or more substances. Table salt dissolved in water is a solution.

Dissolving

When we put certain things like salt or sugar into water, they seem to disappear. In fact, they are still there, but have dissolved.

The plan

We are going to see how temperature affects dissolving.

You will need:

- salt
- small saucepan
- two spoons
- thermometer
- water, stove

What to do:

1 Add salt, one spoonful at a time, to a small saucepan of cold water.

2 Use another spoon to stir the water. Count how many spoonfuls can be added before no more will dissolve.

3 Repeat with the water at different temperatures, using the same quantity of water and same size spoon each time.

4 Leave the hottest one to cool.

What's going on?

The hotter the water, the more salt it can hold in solution. When you let the water cool, the salt cannot stay in solution, and it falls out as salt crystals on the bottom of the pan.

What else can you do?

See if the same thing happens with other solids. You could try different kinds of sugar, sand or even chalk dust!

sand

white sugar

crushed chalk

brown sugar

Jargon Buster

When one substance **dissolves** in another, the result is a **solution**.

Hot air balloon

90 minutes

Here's a demonstration of some of the things we've learned. Getting a balloon off the ground requires a mixture of science and patience!

The plan
We are going to make a balloon powered by hot air.

You will need:

- tissue paper
- card, marker pen, scissors
- glue stick, paper clips
- about 450 mm (18 in) of thin wire
- a hairdryer
- a cardboard or plastic tube (the sort used for mailing posters would do)

What to do:

1 Make a copy of the shape with a blue outline (shown right) on card. You will probably have to stick several sheets together. Make your card 1220 x 280 mm (48 x 11 in), then draw a centre line. Centre each measurement on this line. Draw the outline, then cut it out. This is your *template*.

2 The panels of the balloon are eight pieces of tissue paper 1220 x 280 mm (48 x 11 in). We had to stick sheets of tissue together to make pieces big enough.

3 Make a stack of the eight panels and fasten them together at the corners with paper clips.

4 Lay the card template on the stack. Carefully draw round the template with a marker pen.

28

height = 1220 mm (48 in)

63 mm (2.5 in)

120 mm (4.75)

177 mm (7 in)

221 mm (8.75 in)

253 mm (10 in)

273 mm (10.75 in)

280 mm (11 in)

273 mm (10.75 in)

266 mm (10.5 in)

242 mm (9.5 in)

216 mm (8.5 in)

178 mm (7 in)

146 mm (5.75 in)

114 mm (4.5 in)

50mm (2 in)

75 mm (3 in)

5 Use scissors to cut round your guide line.

7 Use two panels and lay one on top of the other, but about 9 mm (0.375 in) to one side. Put glue on the edge of the lower panel and fold it over the top one.

9 Continue with glueing layers, until you have all eight stuck together. Seen from the end, the stack should look like this*.

diameter: 175 mm (7 in)

6 Cut a circle from tissue, fold in half twice and cut out the V shape.

8 Put on a third piece, moving it 9 mm (0.375 in) back in the opposite direction to the last one. Glue it to the lower one as before.

10 Check there are no parts stuck wrongly. Finish by folding the middle of the stack inwards and out of the way, then glue and fold the last seam.

11 Cut 25mm (1in) deep tabs in the base of each panel.

12 Make a ring from the wire. Fit it inside the neck of the balloon.

fold tabs over wire

13 Wrap the tabs round the ring and glue.

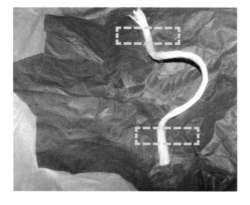

14 Glue the patch on the top. Attach a loop of string with tape.

15 Use a pole to support the balloon.

16 *Inflate* the balloon with the hairdryer and tube. Mend any holes with glue and tissue. Finish filling the balloon.

17 Enjoy the flight!

What's going on?

Hot air expands and is lighter than the surrounding air. When the difference is great enough, it can lift itself and the weight of the balloon that contains it.

Glossary

Blubber	Fat found on sea mammals, especially whales and seals.
Celsius	Scale of temperature measurement most commonly used in science.
Cloud	Mass of vapour, often water, in air.
Conduction	Heat moving from a hotter part of a solid to a cooler part.
Convection	The movement of heat through a liquid or gas caused by hot material rising.
Cycle	A series of events that repeat themselves in the same order.
Diameter	The measurement across a circle.
Dissolve	To mix a substance with a liquid so that they become a solution.
Evaporation	Turning from a liquid to a vapour.
Freeze	Turn from a liquid to a solid by lowering temperature.
Iceberg	Large mass of ice floating in the sea.
Inflate	Fill with a gas, usually air.
Insulator	Something that prevents loss of heat.
Margarine	Spread used instead of butter, made from vegetable oils and animal fats.
Radiation	A form of heat energy spread by rays or waves. Radiation can travel through a vacuum.
Smoke	Tiny particles, mostly carbon, distributed through the air.
Spiral	A gradually widening and continuous curve around a central point.
Stretchies	A stretchy band used to hold up long hair.
Temperature	The degree or intensity of heat present in a substance.
Template	Sometimes called a pattern, a template is a guide for making lots of things the same shape. There is one on page 29, to make the panels for the hot air balloon.
Thermometer	A device for measuring temperature.
Vacuum	Space containing absolutely nothing.

Index

Websites

http://www.sciencekidsathome.com/
http://www.abc.net.au/spark/experiments/list.htm
http://kids.nationalgeographic.com/Activities/FunScience
http://kids-science-experiments.com/